Jahari's Adventure

Tales from the Serengeti

Jahari was a young zebra of fairly **short** stature. The tip of his nose merely rose to his mother's striped side which he found **very frustrating**.

Because he was
still quite young,
his size was
perfectly
normal, as his
mother often
reminded him.

"**DUST, HOOVES** and **TAILS** is **ALL** that I see!" complained Jahari to anyone who would listen, or just happened to be around.

"This herd is not suitable for those of our **size**," he continued to the wildebeest twins. "We shall start a new herd of our own kind—the short and the small."

"I'm sorry but you must **stay** with us," chanted their mothers all together. "You must understand that the herd is for **safety**, not meant for sightseeing."

But none of the
youngsters heeded
their mothers'
wise words.

That night the
small group slipped
silently away,
all on their
own.

The next day they
found themselves some
distance from the
main herd.
Still the little troop
carried on,
laughing
and
enjoying
all the new sights
and sounds.

Nobody paid any
attention to where
they were going.

Suddenly, Jahari
and the others
came to an abrupt
HALT.
Everything was
quiet and still
because they had
stumbled
right into the middle
of a resting
pride of lions!

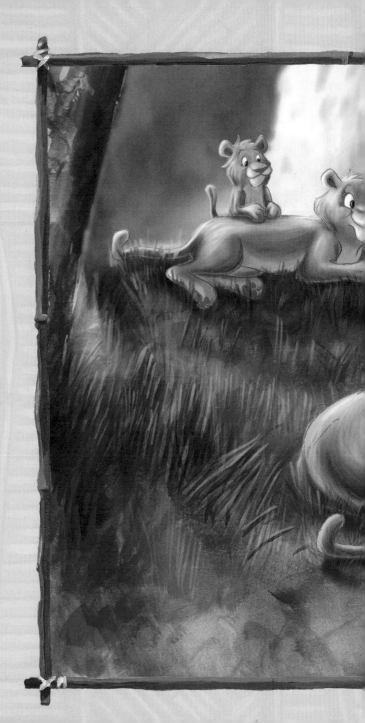

"Aahhhhhh!" they yelped. In a *f l a s h* the friends were gone, as–fast–as their little legs could take them. The lions didn't even realize what was going on!

Once Jahari and his
friends were safely back
with the herd, they
apologized
for disobeying.
The herd welcomed
them back and made
a new rule:
All short and small
animals could run at the
front of the herd.

Jahari was now a
very **happy** zebra.